When Cat and Rat Were Friends

A Folktale from Africa

Cat and Rat were best friends. In the rainy season, Cat built a home. He shared it with Rat. In the hungry season, Rat shared his food with Cat. In the dry season, Rat and Cat looked for water together. They drank lemon tea together.

Cat and Rat were always together. The other animals said their names together. It was like one name.

One sunny day, Hippo and Deer were together by the river. They were talking. "Catandrat make a lovely pair," said Hippo.

"They do!" said Deer. She stretched her neck. She wanted a closer look. "Cat has bright green eyes. Rat has a handsome gray coat. They look wonderful together."

Cat and Rat didn't mind. It was fine with them to have their names said together. They were proud of their friendship. They were happy to be called Catandrat.

One day Cat made some soup with *fufu*. Rat and Cat were sharing the soup. Rat had an idea. He said, "My dear friend, Cat! We can grow *cassava*. Let's make a cassava farm together. Then we will have a lot of cassava plants. We can roast the cassava. We can boil it. We can fry it. We can even bake the cassava! Cat, we will never be hungry again. And we can sell what we don't eat. Then we'll share the money."

"What a wonderful idea, Rat!" said Cat. "There are two of us to do the work. We will have lots of cassava."

"And lots of money," said Rat.

The two friends started a cassava farm. They cleared the field together. They burned the bush together. They got the ground ready, and they planted the cassava together. In the long, hot growing season, they weeded the farm together.

It was hard work. But Cat and Rat didn't complain. Cat talked about cooking. He talked about ways to cook cassava. Rat talked about selling cassava. He wanted money to spend.

"I will make us roasted cassava, fried cassava, and my delicious soup with fufu," said Cat.

"Then we will sell the rest of the cassava in the city," said Rat.

"Why will we go to the city?" asked Cat. "It costs a lot to live in the city, Rat."

Rat said, "I want to go there. We can buy fine clothes. We can eat in grand restaurants. We can be seen with the right people."

Rat looked at Cat. He knew Cat was not happy.

Rat said, "I know restaurant fufu soup won't be as good as yours, Cat. But it would be fun to eat in a restaurant."

"I guess so," said Cat. He didn't like to argue.

Rat knew it cost a lot to visit the city. But he had a plan.

One day it was almost time to harvest the cassava. Rat sold all the cassava to Leopard. Then he ran away to the city. He was never seen again.

When Rat didn't come to harvest the
cassava, Cat was worried. He looked
for his friend in the bush. No one had
seen Rat for days. Cat went back to the
cassava farm. He would harvest the
crop of cassava by himself.

Imagine Cat's surprise! He saw Leopard taking the cassava.

"What are you doing, Leopard?" cried Cat.

"It's MY cassava," Leopard said. "Rat sold it to me. Then he went to the city."

Cat was angry. He knew he had been tricked. After that, Cat chased any rat he saw. The rat just might be his old double-crossing friend.

And, to this day, that is why cats always chase rats.